Thistle Gets Hurt

Lady Thistle, the Horse

D.H. ANDERSON
Illustrations by **STEVEN LESTER**

Thistle Gets Hurt

Paperback ISBN 978-1-960007-26-1
HardBack ISBN 978-1-960007-25-4
eBOOK ISBN 978-1-960007-27-8

Published by
Little Blessing Books
an imprint of
Orison Publishers, Inc.
PO Box 188, Grantham, PA 17027
www.OrisonPublishers.com

Acknowledgments

Contributing Veterinarian: Apryle Horbal, VMD

Dedication
To Wynter Snowflake,
Yanik and Salem

It is two months since Lady Thistle was born at Waterdam Farm, and she is growing fast! She eats grain and grass and drinks cool, fresh water like a big horse, but it is still important for her to drink her mother's milk. Everyone watches closely to keep this curious little filly away from lurking dangers.

Each morning, Polly and Thistle eat their grain. Thistle eats quickly and then tries to eat from her mother's wall feeder; she wants more, but Polly is firm and does not let her eat too much.

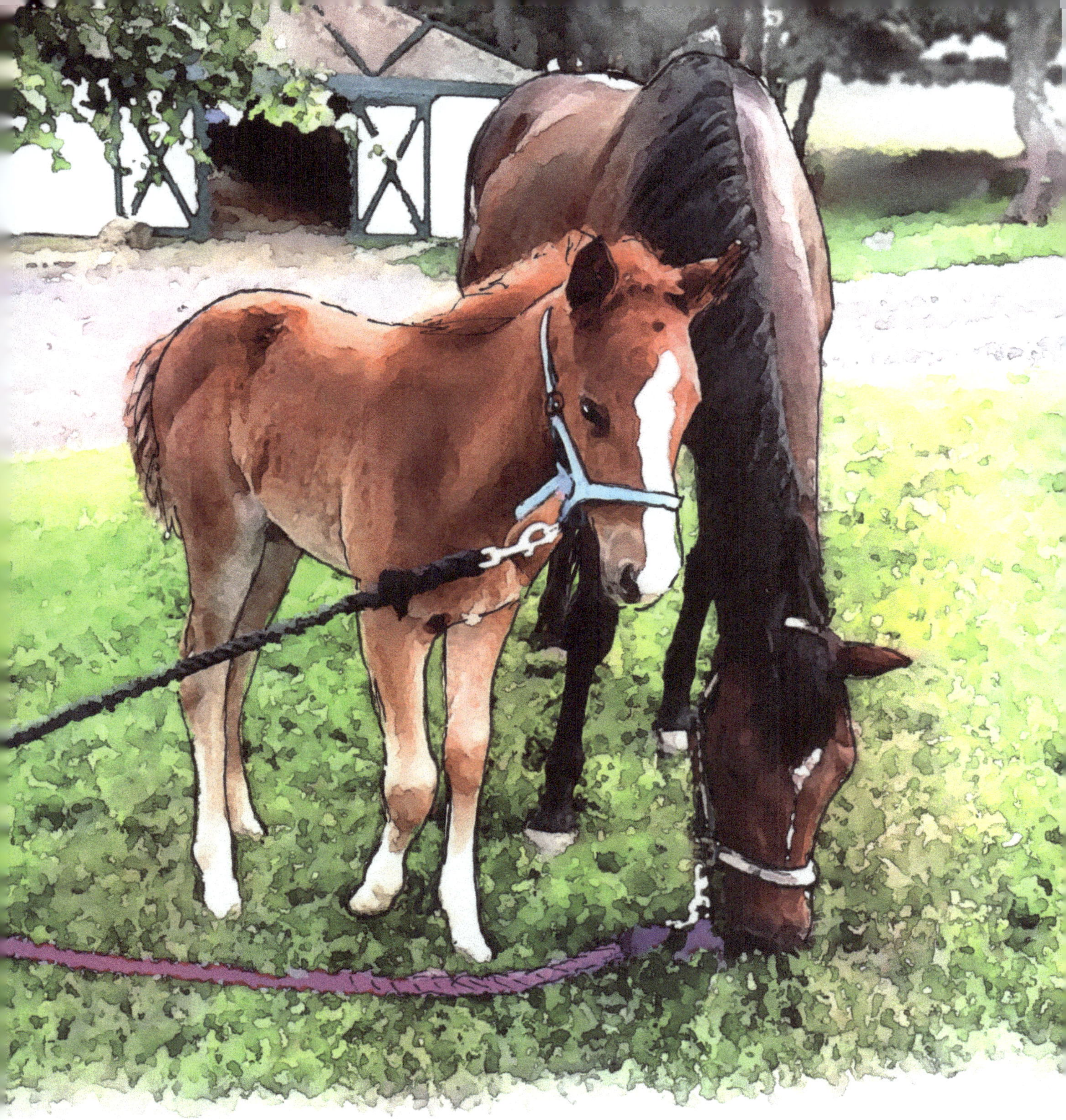

Polly and Thistle walk to the field on lead ropes. Dr. Apryle has decided that Polly, Thistle, and Daphne should share a field, while Wynter joins Lite in another field.

5

The horses all enjoy their outside time; they eat grass and sweet, green clover, seek shade under the trees, and run and play.

Thistle gets after Polly to nurse, but then she kicks up her legs, and off they run, round and round the field! Friends and family laugh as they watch young Lady Thistle!

This is a good time to clean stalls, place fresh hay, fill the buckets with water, and make repairs on the doors and walls, because horses can do damage that might cause an injury.

Midday, the horses return to the stable for a rest from the summer sun. A large fan in the barn provides a continuous breeze.

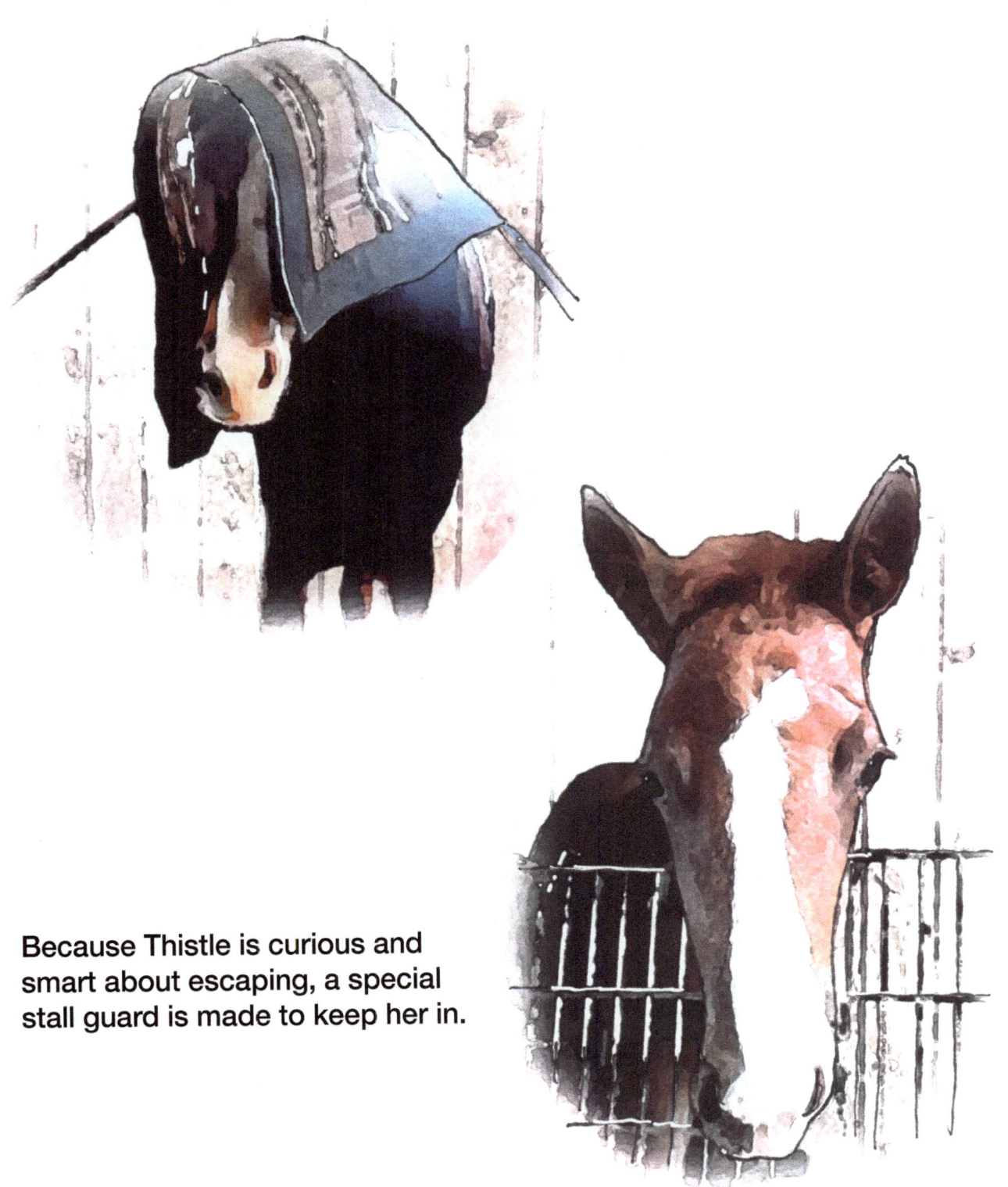

Because Thistle is curious and smart about escaping, a special stall guard is made to keep her in.

One day, after leading the horses outside for the morning, the farmhands hear loud shrieks coming from the field. They run back and see Polly at the fence. She rears up, telling them that something is terribly wrong.

They see little Thistle hobbling toward them. OH NO! She has a big cut, and they see blood running down her leg! She is having trouble walking because it hurts so much. She is beginning to panic. Polly whinnies, asking for help!

The farmhands call the family's mom. Then they slowly approach Polly and Thistle to place their halters on, so they can get them to the safety of the barn. They comfort Lady Thistle. Even though Polly is upset too, she shows Thistle how to let them help. The men slowly lead Polly and Thistle out of the field.

Mom sees that the cut is bad. It runs the entire length of Thistle's lower leg. What should be done first? She tries to rinse the cut with water, but this makes Thistle panic more. Mom calls Dr. Apryle, who, luckily, can come immediately. She says to get Thistle to stand still but do nothing else until she arrives.

13

Polly and Thistle's farm friends are worried—they wonder how the filly cut her leg. Daphne, Wynter, and Lite call from the fields to be taken into the barn. They want to be close to little Thistle. Yanik takes his place at the barn door, and the cats gather in a circle around their frightened baby friend.

Dr. Apryle arrives and looks at Thistle's cut. It is very long and needs stitches. It is good that Thistle's knee and ankle joints were not injured. Dr. Apryle is still worried, though. She needs to clean the cut well to prevent an infection, but Thistle does not want anyone to touch her leg!

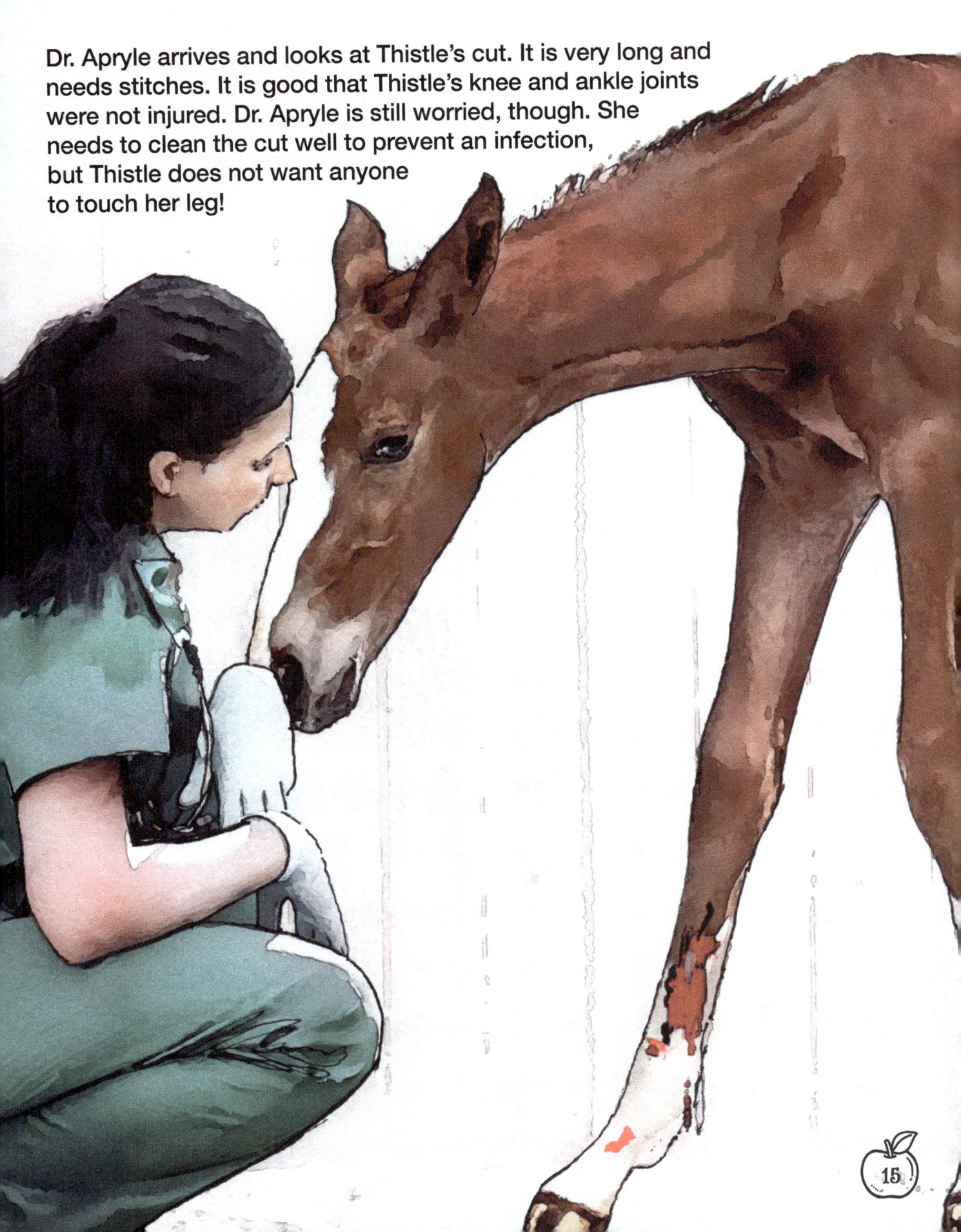

Dr. Apryle injects some medicine into Thistle's neck to help her relax. The medicine makes Thistle sleepy, but a horse should stand to be treated for a cut like this. The farmhands help to steady her. Now, Thistle is ready to let Dr. Apryle work on her leg. Taylor, a vet tech, has arrived and will assist.

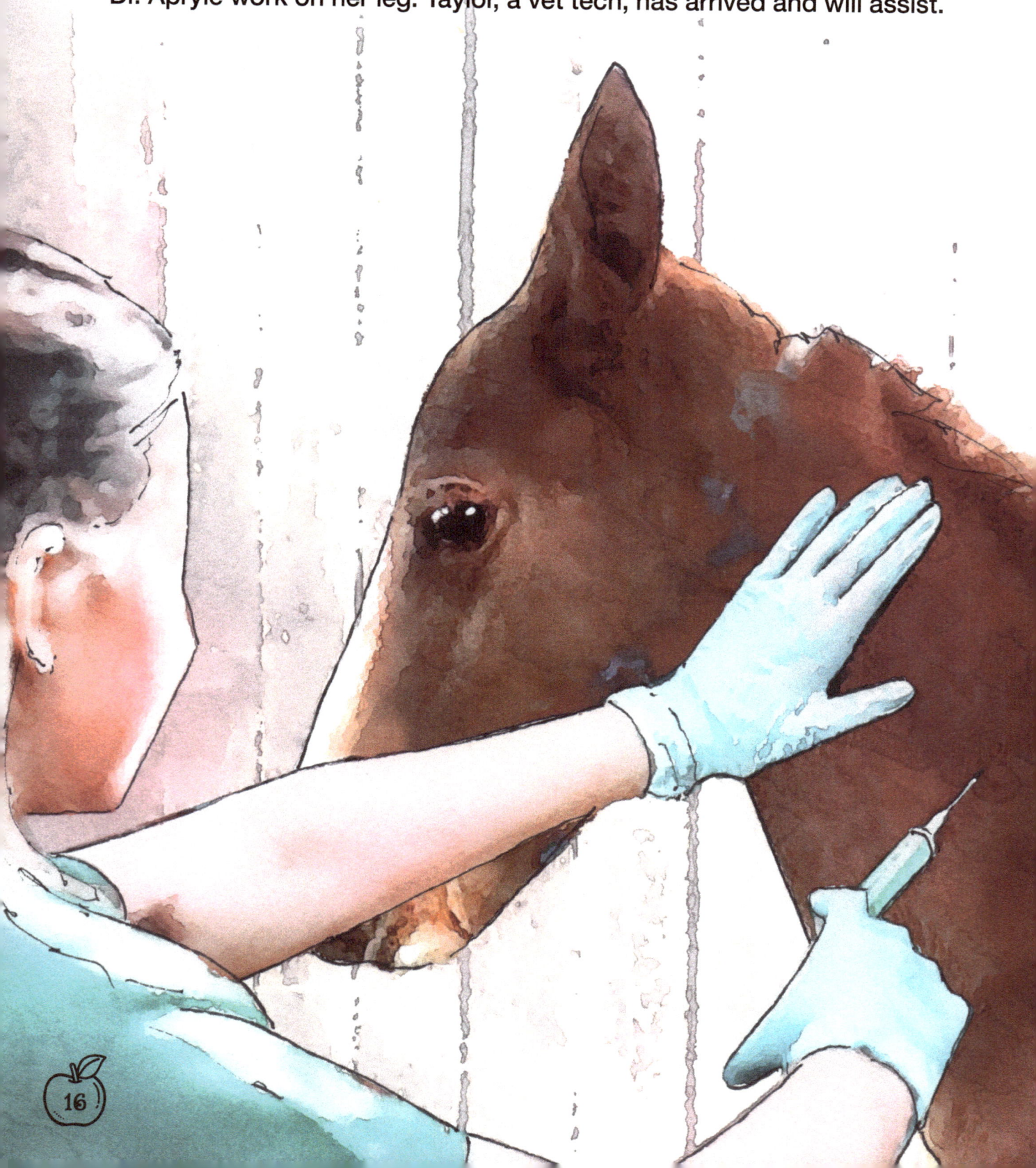

They rinse the cut with water and clean it with a special medical soap. This cleaning takes a long time, but veterinarians know how important it is that horses do not get infections.

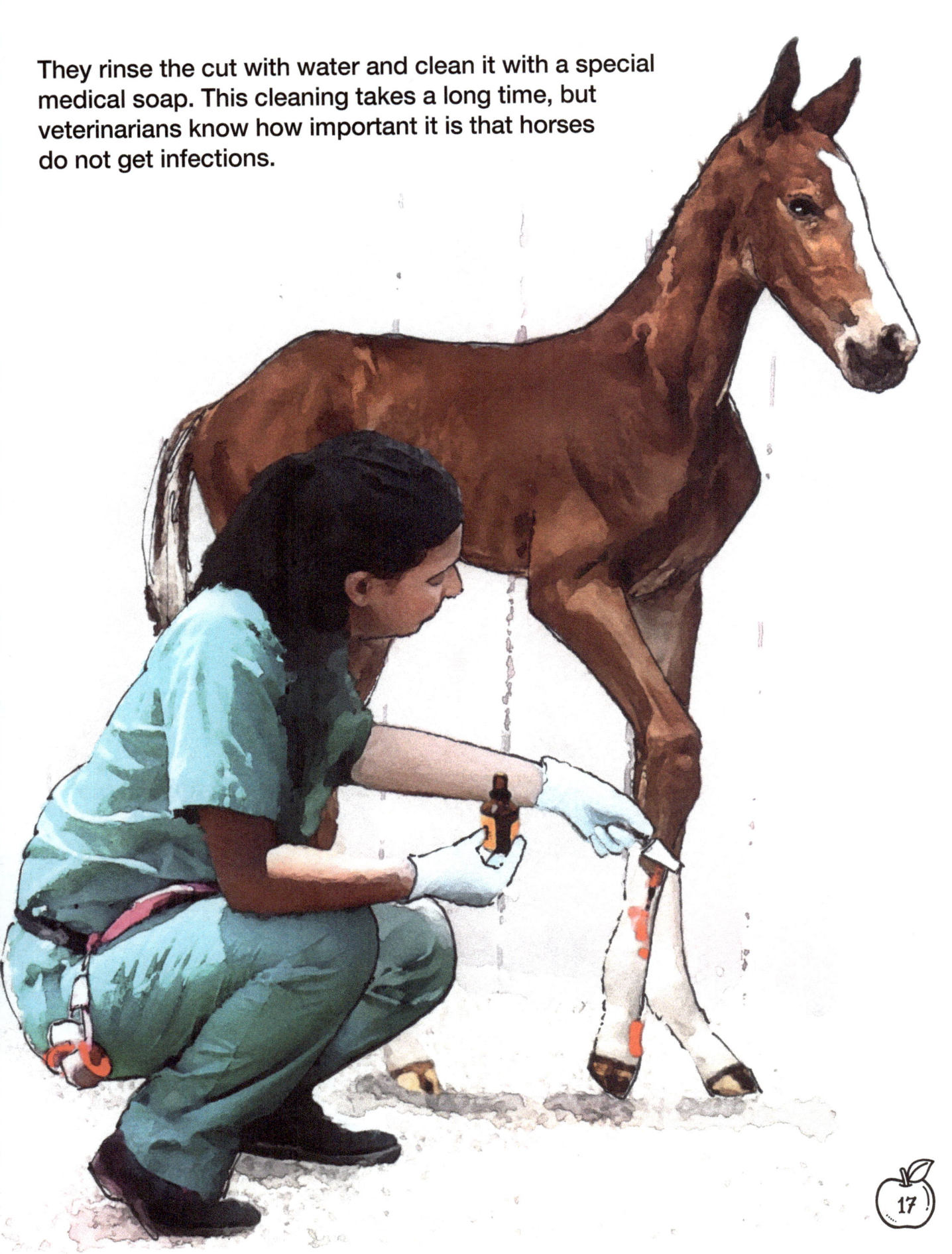

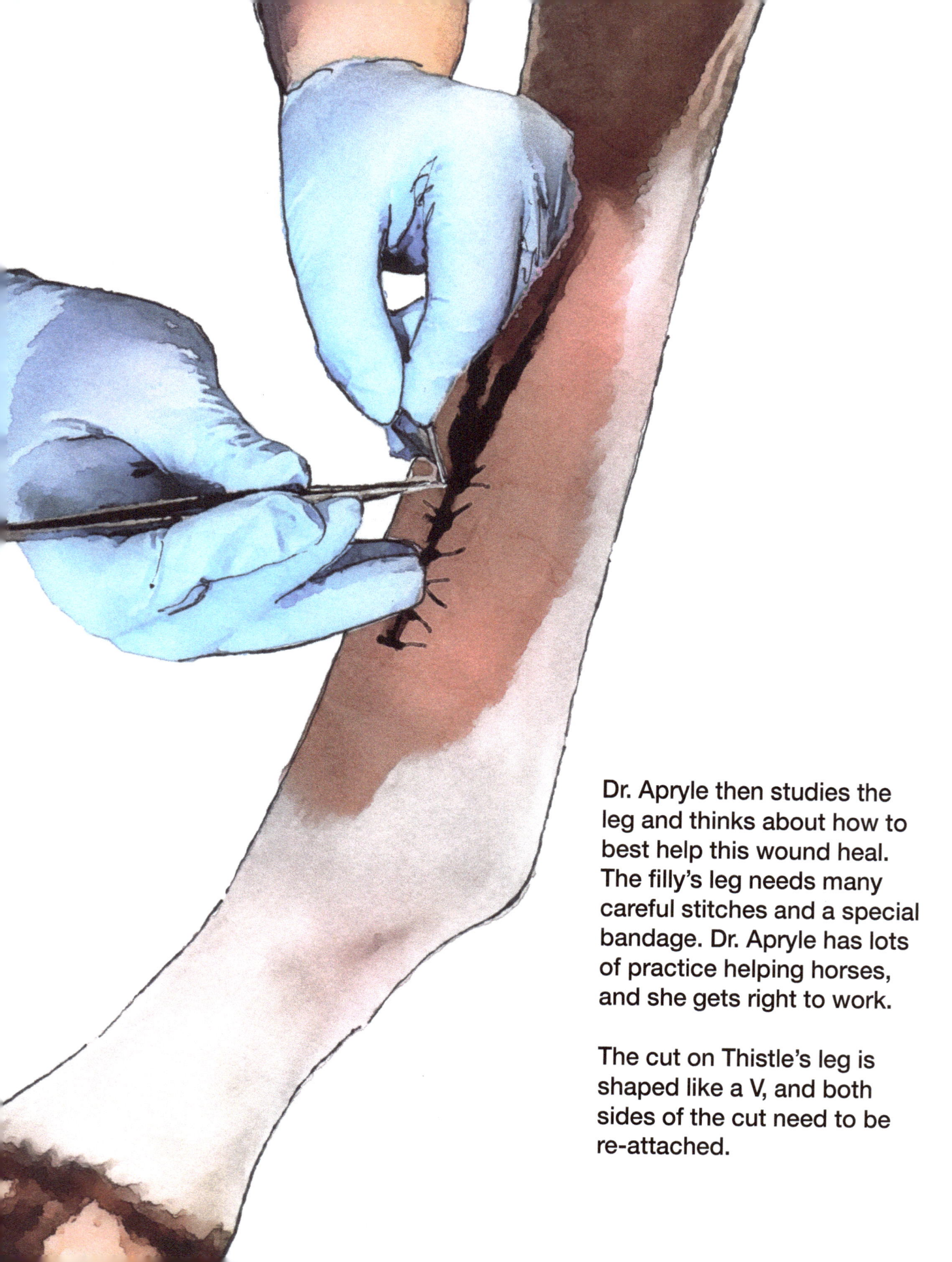

Dr. Apryle then studies the leg and thinks about how to best help this wound heal. The filly's leg needs many careful stitches and a special bandage. Dr. Apryle has lots of practice helping horses, and she gets right to work.

The cut on Thistle's leg is shaped like a V, and both sides of the cut need to be re-attached.

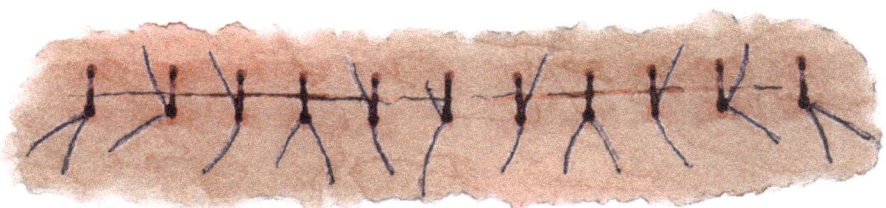

Each tiny stitch must be carefully placed with a curved needle and secured with "sutures," which are special strings. After an hour of stitching, Dr. Apryle needs a rest.

Another hour later, the stitches are complete, and she wraps a bandage around the leg.

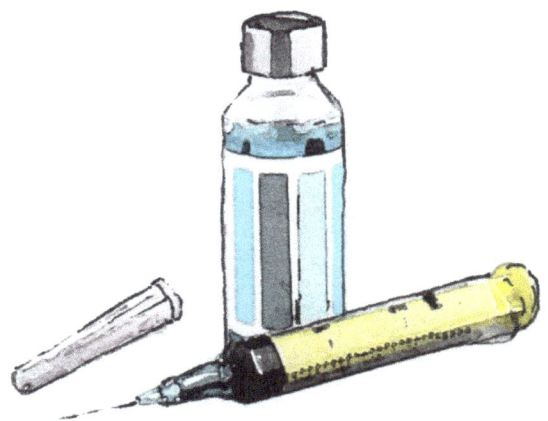

Dr. Apryle injects medicine into Thistle's big neck muscle to help prevent infection.

Polly and Thistle are frightened, but they know to trust Dr. Apryle and the others. Once the horses have their grain, hay, and water, the barn is closed for the night. Every so often, there is a soft nicker as one of the horses checks to see if Thistle is okay. She answers softly with her tiny, high-pitched nicker.

The next day, Dr. Apryle arrives early to make sure Thistle can stand and nurse. Then she leads Thistle out of her stall and gives her medicine to help her relax. She takes off the bandage and cleans the cut again. The stitches look good, and she puts on a fresh bandage.

Thistle and Polly stay in. As Wynter, Daphne and Lite are walking out, they nicker to Thistle as if to say, "Feel better!"

The family wonders how baby Thistle hurt her leg so badly.
They search the field for

a broken fence,

a sharp edge on the run in,

a tree stump,

but find nothing.

Then, while putting some hay in the field, they see the culprit. A plastic storm pipe hit by a mower has a sharp edge.

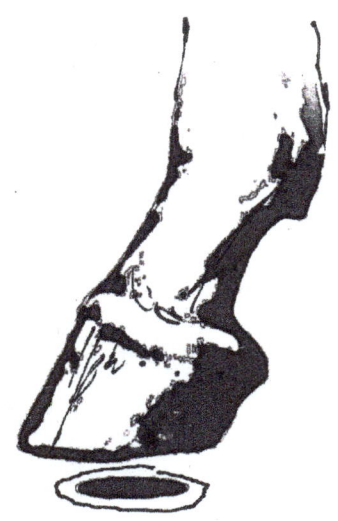

Grown-up horses' hooves are bigger than the pipe, but not baby Thistle's. Her hoof slid right into the pipe, and the sharp edge cut her delicate leg.

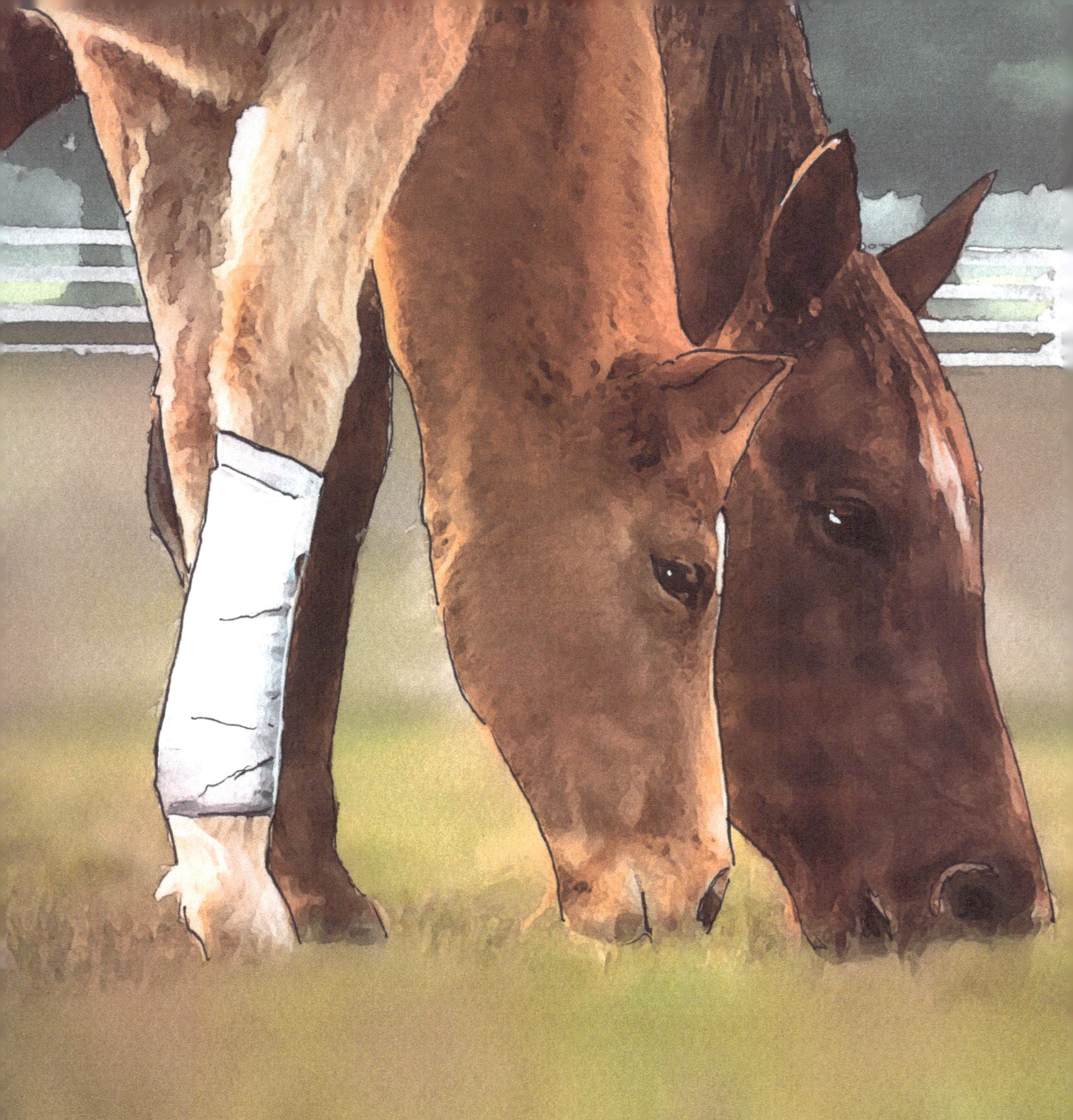

Dr. Apryle changes Thistle's bandage each day. After a few days of healing, Thistle and Polly go outside on their lead ropes for a bit of grass. But fun in the fields will have to wait.

After several weeks of healing, Thistle and Polly finally get Dr. Apryle's okay to spend a few hours in the pasture. The farm family and all of Thistle's friends are relieved to see her outdoors nursing, grazing, and happy!

The Waterdam Farm family checks on Thistle one last time for the day.

And then, comforted that all is well, they head home for the night, leaving the stable to the soothing sound of the continuous munching of hay.

Did You Know...?

Horses stand for most medical treatments. Sometimes a horse has to lie down with the help of medications. But when that sleep medicine wears off, the horse might panic and try to get up too quickly. That's dangerous for the horse and for the people around it. That's why veterinarians work with the horse standing whenever possible.

Horses can sleep lightly while standing up for short periods. Their bodies have a "stay apparatus" involving the ligaments, muscles, tendons, and the joints of the legs that lets them keep their balance with very little effort. Since horses can't rise quickly from the ground because they are so big, the ability to sleep standing up helps them escape predators in the wild.

When a horse gets a cut or a scrape, it is very important to clean the wound thoroughly, especially if it is around one of the leg joints. Antibiotics can help prevent or treat infection. They can be given by mouth, injected, or put right on the wound, especially if it is on or near a joint.

To keep horses healthy, their stalls should be cleaned every day. Removing manure and other dirt helps prevent the spread of diseases, and it keeps bugs away.

Every day, horses need fresh water in a clean bucket. They also need fresh hay that has been checked for mold. Bad hay lacks color and has a lot of dust. Sometimes it smells moldy, or you can see black mold on it. The hay also must be checked for foreign objects that could give the horse colic (a stomachache) or hurt its mouth. Good hay provides nutrients and is high in fiber, which keep the horse's digestive system healthy. There are many types of hay, and what horses eat often depends on where they live. Some common hays where Thistle lives are made of timothy, alfalfa, and orchard grasses.

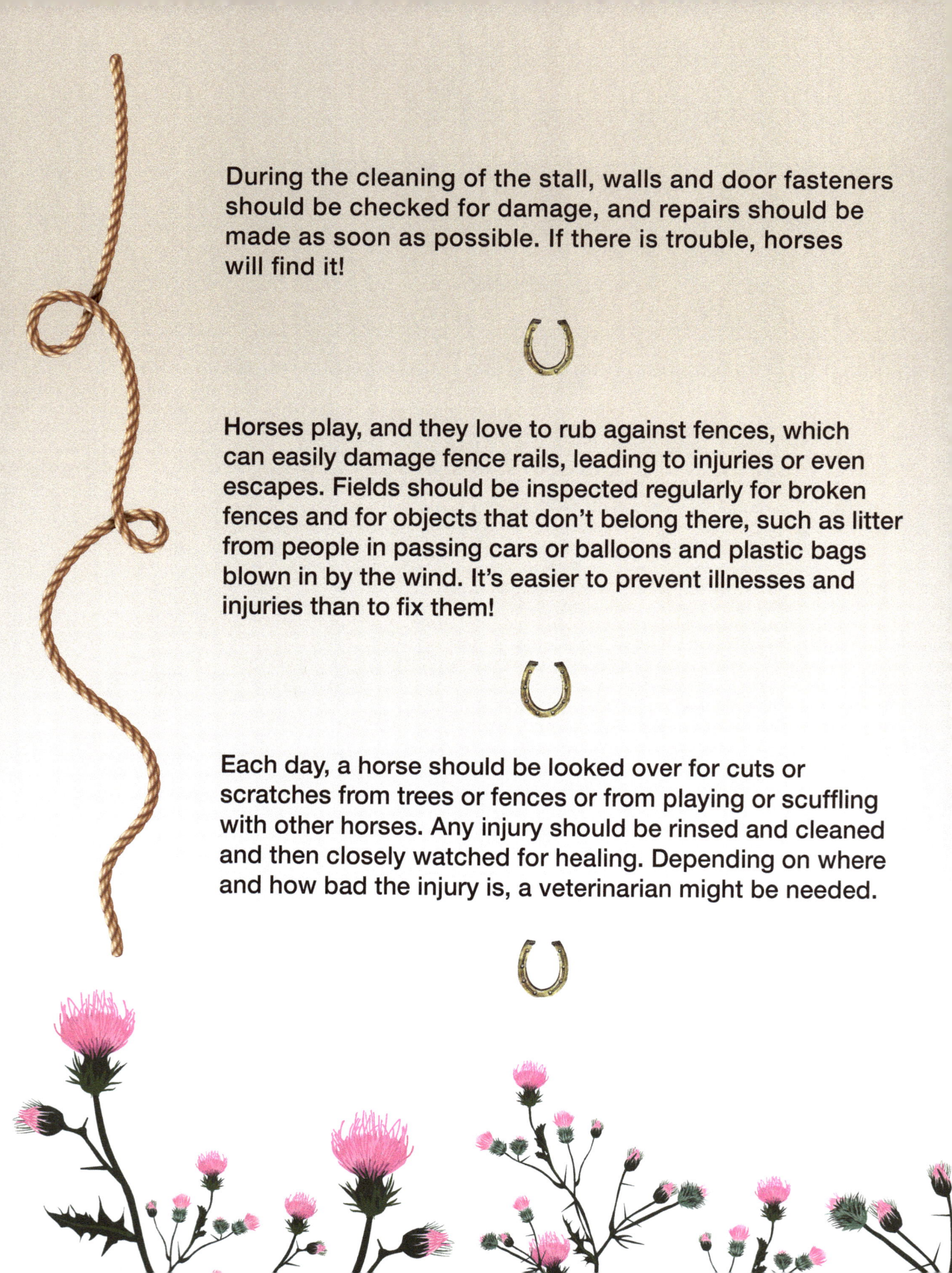

During the cleaning of the stall, walls and door fasteners should be checked for damage, and repairs should be made as soon as possible. If there is trouble, horses will find it!

Horses play, and they love to rub against fences, which can easily damage fence rails, leading to injuries or even escapes. Fields should be inspected regularly for broken fences and for objects that don't belong there, such as litter from people in passing cars or balloons and plastic bags blown in by the wind. It's easier to prevent illnesses and injuries than to fix them!

Each day, a horse should be looked over for cuts or scratches from trees or fences or from playing or scuffling with other horses. Any injury should be rinsed and cleaned and then closely watched for healing. Depending on where and how bad the injury is, a veterinarian might be needed.

Polly and the Birth Day

D.H. ANDERSON
Illustrations by STEVEN LESTER

Thistle and Her First Day

D.H. ANDERSON
Illustrations by STEVEN LESTER

Thistle Starts Exploring

D.H. ANDERSON
Illustrations by STEVEN LESTER

Thistle Gets Hurt

D.H. ANDERSON
Illustrations by STEVEN LESTER

Watch for Lady Thistle's Journey to continue.

SCAN ME